How to Write a Story:

an alternative approach using the subconscious

– evolution meets storytelling

by
PAUL LARKIN

ISBN: 978-0-244-16981-7

CONTENTS

Chapter 9
PUTTING IT ALL TOGETHER

TERMINOLOGY

INTRODUCTION

Why I wrote this book

There were two major factors that inspired me to write *How to Write a Story: an alternative approach using the subconscious.*

First Factor: Different topics, same story

The first factor that inspired me was listening to the speakers at several 'How to Get Rich' seminars. While the topics varied from cryptocurrency to property, the presenter's introduction was always the same. They began by telling us how poor they were or how they dreamed of being rich. Then they started their journey to riches. At first everything went wrong and they lost lots of money. But they persisted, struggled and climbed out of debt. Now they are millionaires. Their journey took them down and then up.

Second Factor: Different centuries, same experience

The second factor that inspired me was the book by Anne Baring called *The Dream of the Cosmos*. She researched the influence of Nature on the human psyche. The Moon changed shape throughout the month; it would disappear then re-appear. For thousands of years mankind saw the full moon, then the half-moon then the quarter moon, only to disappear then appear again as a quarter moon, half-moon and so on.

There was another lesson from Nature. Seeds and bulbs were buried. They disappeared under the earth. However, they would struggle and reappear. They would grow and reach full bloom. Mankind would see this cycle for thousands of years. It became part of the human psyche. It became the pattern of life. Nature struggled. Mankind struggled. But with persistence came success.

Patterns and your audience

The basis of this book is the pattern that was burned into mankind's subconscious. Carl Jung, the psychiatrist, describes it as the 'collective unconscious'. It is part of your make-up and that of your audience's. Your audience has this innate understanding of struggle, the journey from where you are, through a maze of challenges until finally you achieve success. If you use this pattern, you will relate to every member of your audience. You will get their attention and hold their interest.

Do you have to come up with original ideas? – No. They are out there already!

If you wanted to, you could spend hours coming up with an original story. Then, by trial and error, you could test its success by the response of your audience.

Or, you could use the elements of stories that have proved successful over thousands of years. There is a quick and easy way to build a story that gets your audience's attention and holds their interest. The elements are:

PLOTS – there are certain major problems that have been favourites for centuries
MOTIVATION – there are certain minor problems that keep your audience interested

CONFLICT – physical conflict captures attention, but there are more subtle ways

PEOPLE – popular characters are found in ever successful story

WORDS – particular words involve your audience more than others.

These elements are identified throughout the book. They will help you to create a stunning story both quickly and easily.

What you will learn as you read this book

You will learn not only what works in a successful story but also why it works. You will meet neuroscience, philosophy and psychology. You will see how these fields of study join forces with literary analysis. You will discover:

- The five major plots that guide your story from beginning to end. Discover the major problems that all audiences can relate to. You will know the direction of your story as soon as you start creating.

- The seven characters that find their way into every story. You will know immediately how these characters should act, what they should say and what they should look like. Your audience will identify with these characters immediately.

- The five minor plots that guarantee interest. Selecting smaller challenges that activate your hero becomes easy. Select one of the standard minor challenges and your story gains momentum. Want to make your story even longer? You just add more minor problems.

- Words to avoid. There are words and phrases that are taboo. Learn the vocabulary that appeals to your audience and grabs their attention immediately. The right choice of words has the audience under your spell.

- The two types of conflict. Physical conflict gets attention but there is another situation that audiences love. It's subtle, it's used in the top-selling movies and novels. You'll discover how you can use it.

Conclusion

How to Write a Story: an alternative approach using the subconscious is a book that helps you to create stories that will get your audience's attention. It ensures your success as a writer. In this book, you are given the elements of a great story. You will learn why those elements are successful. You will be guided in your story-telling journey.

Chapter 1

STRUCTURE: your story needs a *down–struggle– up* pattern

In evolutionary terms, mankind has only recently learned how to talk. Some scientists suggest it was approximately 40,000–20,000 BC when humans developed the vocal tract, larynx, tongue and mouth coordination needed to form words and a language. Then, around 3000 BC, they developed the first examples of written language. What was man mentally recording before he could use words? What experiences influenced his early stories? The purpose of this book is to answer these questions.

What did man see before he could say?

Over the millions of years of evolution, humans would have seen cycles in Nature. The seasons would have changed. Plant life would have flourished, died then sprouted again.

What influence did the Moon have on mankind?

Despite street lights, headlights and house lamps, the Moon is still very obvious. Imagine how bright it would have been before cities and towns existed. Early man would have seen this bright circle in the sky. Over time, it would shrink to half size then quarter size. It would disappear. It would reappear then go back through the cycle to full size. It was as if the Moon were becoming weaker and weaker then apparently dying before rising again to full glory. Life–death–life was a theme that every generation would have seen many times. The pattern of down–struggle–up was being registered in the psyche of mankind.

What influence did plants have on mankind?

As mankind moved to a more agricultural existence, humans would have buried seeds and vegetables. The seeds would fight their way to the surface. They would grow. They would then flourish as crops grew ready for harvest. Vegetables were covered with soil. Within months, they would struggle to the surface, sprout vegetation and produce food. Nature was continually telling mankind that he will succeed when he struggles and persists, despite apparent obstacles. Struggle, obstacles and success became a theme that mankind experienced frequently.

How did Nature influence mankind's storytelling?

a) Moon cycle:

The Moon went through a cycle of full life, half-life, quarter-life, death . . . then quarter-life, half-life, full life.

In story terms, your audience can accept that your hero can:
- experience failure but will eventually succeed
- seemingly die but will eventually rise again.

b) plant cycle:

Seeds and vegetables were buried under the earth. They fought their way to the surface. They grew. They succeeded and flourished.

In story terms, your audience can accept that your hero can:
- feel overwhelmed but, if they are determined, they will succeed
- be seemingly defeated but, if they struggle and persevere, they will be successful.

How do you use these findings in your storytelling?

You and your audience are born with an understanding of these cycles in Nature. It is implanted in mankind's psyche. If you use the memories in the collective unconscious, you will understand Nature's patterns. Your stories will reflect this. Your audience will understand you. You will be a success.

Combining all these findings into a story pattern:
- *Character experiences failure but will eventually succeed.*
- *Character is seemingly defeated, but if they struggle and persevere, they will be successful.*

Your story will appeal to your audience if your main character:

- wants to achieve something (pleasure) or avoid something (pain)
- experiences obstacles that get worse and worse

- struggles and perseveres
- experiences events that get better and better
- succeeds.

Can you give me an example?

For example, your hero wants more money and better career prospects (pleasure).

- Hero applies for a job. Gets interview
- Hero uses car to go for interview – car will not start
- Hero calls for car assistance – will not arrive before interview time
- Hero rushes to train station – train cancelled
- Hero about to use mobile phone to tell interviewer he will be late but the battery is flat
- Hero gets taxi – arrives on time
- Hero studies notes in preparation – spills coffee on them
- Hero gets interview – just says what is on his mind without notes
- Hero asked to leave interview session and wait in reception
- Hero informed he has got the job
- Hero starts job
- Hero gets promoted and more money.

Conclusion

In this example, you should get the feel of how things went from bad to worse. Character struggles and perseveres then things get better and better. It all ends in success. This is the down–struggle–up pattern that mankind has experienced for millions of years. If you use it in your storytelling, you will be successful.

Chapter 2

PLOT: major events that caused action

In the previous chapter you saw an example of a story pattern that was inspired by Nature. The pattern was modelled on down–struggle–up.

In the example given, the character wanted more money and better career prospects. The emphasis was on gaining pleasure (getting more money to buy luxury items) rather than on avoiding pain (losing a job and having no money to survive).

Why do humans change their behaviour?

Human beings will act only when they really want something (pleasure) or they really want to avoid something (pain). Mediocrity is not an option in your story. Your character must earnestly want something – be it to gain pleasure or to avoid pain.

The two major problems that produce action are:
a) wanting something (pleasure)
b) not wanting something (pain).

Five major events that caused mankind pleasure or pain – and resulted in action

There were five major causes of pleasure or pain throughout history. Every human being experienced them, and they were recorded in mankind's psyche. You have inherited that psyche in what Carl Jung calls the 'Collective Unconscious'. These events resonate with you and your audience. The five major events that your audience can relate to are:

1 Person leaves home to achieve a goal that benefits others, then returns home

At one stage, early humans were few and far between. They were independent units. A common and traumatic experience that parents faced was providing food for the family. Mother or father would leave their loved ones and go into the wilderness. They would encounter wild beasts or hostile terrain to procure the necessary food then they would return home. Seeing their family again would have registered in their psyche. The reward of the kill would have added to their happiness (pleasure) and reinforced the memory.

The major event that caused action =
need to leave home, achieve a goal for the benefit of others, return home.

Remember, in this chapter you are identifying the major event that caused action. At this point, you are not concerned with minor details or descriptions.

2 Present situation ends, person has to adapt to a new situation

Regardless of the era, families have experienced floods, droughts, and fires. They have had to abandon their homes and move on. Their previous life ended, and they had to start anew.

The emphasis was on seeking a new existence. Humans were seeking an alternative situation. They realised that their life would not be the same. They would have to adapt to a new way of living. Change was forced on them and they had to adapt. These events were inscribed on mankind's psyche. You and your audience have inherited the memory.

The major event that caused action =
present situation ends, need to adapt to a new situation.

Remember, in this chapter you are identifying the major event that caused action. At this point, you are not concerned with minor details or descriptions.

3 Person has to fight an enemy in order to protect the tribe

As more and more humans populated the earth, they grouped together to form tribes. The father-mother-children unit still existed. Parents would protect their own family from danger but now there was a need for someone to protect the whole tribe.

The Hero appeared. The Hero would fight the demon and save the tribe. So popular was this theme that heroes had their exploits exaggerated and tribe members would make these stories part of their memories. You and your audience have inherited this pattern.

The major event that caused action =
need to fight the enemy and save the tribe.

4 Person needs to be less selfish and contribute more to the tribe

Joseph Campbell, in his work *The Hero with a Thousand Faces,* researched primitive tribes and their customs. He found that all of them had some sort of initiation ceremony. A child was part of the tribe but made little contribution to its welfare. This was acceptable until adolescence then the youth was taken from its mother. The elders would subject the child to various ordeals. Alone and facing danger, the child was transformed into an adult. The tribe welcomed him back but expected him to be a contributing member to the group. The candidate was no longer a child.

The major event that caused action =
reduce selfishness and increase contribution to the tribe.

Remember, in this chapter you are identifying the major event that caused action. At this point, you are not concerned with minor details or descriptions.

5 Person wants to be rich and have a better life

As tribes developed, so did the desire to assert their superiority. The richer and more powerful the tribe, the more that tribe could dominate other tribes.

Individuals within the tribe saw their status rise as they acquired wealth. The desire to be rich became an incentive to have a better life. The dream of being wealthy was fixed firmly in mankind's psyche. It meant pleasure and happiness.

The major event that caused action =
desire to be rich and have a better life.

Remember, in this chapter you are identifying the major event that caused action. At this point, you are not concerned with minor details or descriptions.

Conclusion

The major problems that caused early mankind to act are:

1 Person leaves home to achieve a goal for the benefit of others, then returns home
2 Present situation ends, person has to adapt to a new situation
3 Person needs to fight an enemy to protect the tribe
4 Person needs to be less selfish and contribute more to the tribe
5 Person wants to be rich and have a better life

These major events forced early mankind to act. Your audience is aware of them and has experienced variations on them. For example, the father no longer leaves their family to hunt for food, but he does leave his family to go to work and earn money to buy food. There is a parallel. Similarly, an army general leads his troops to fight the enemy and protect the nation. The entrepreneur works hard to rise out of poverty and experience a better life.

The events of the past are part of the present. Being aware of the major events that mankind has faced makes the creation of your story easier. You now know the easy way to start the action of your story. You have been given the secret. Use this knowledge to start an action-packed story that your audience can relate to.

Chapter 3

MINOR PLOTS: needs cause action

In the previous chapter, you met major problems that early mankind faced. These major problems ensured action. The major problem gives your story direction: it indicates the beginning and the end.

The middle needs some minor struggles. These struggles maintain your audience's interest.

What else makes humans do something?

People act when they either want to gain something (pleasure) or avoid something (pain). When the promise of pleasure is great enough, the person will act. If the threat of pain is great enough, the person will act. Action and a change of behaviour depend on pleasure or pain.

Psychologists have studied human behaviour and tried to identify what causes humans to act. They wanted to know what causes humans to feel pleasure or to feel pain.

What did the psychologist called Maslow have to offer?

Abraham Maslow investigated the sources of pain. These included hunger, loneliness, lack of respect.

He researched what a person would do to relieve that pain. What action would they take to achieve pleasure? Maslow was more interested in behaviour to achieve pleasure. If the pain was hunger, the human would perform action to attain the pleasure of food. The action taken was caused by the need to have food.

Hunger (pain) causes a person to seek (action) some kind of food (need) and eliminate hunger (pleasure). 'Food' – need for food – hunger. Maslow reverses the pain/pleasure arrangement.

Are there any other pains that cause a person to act?

The factors that cause pain are many, but most psychologists refer to the rewards (pleasure) e.g. food, shelter, affection and so on. Maslow took what he considered to be the most important pains and analysed their pain-pleasure relationship. Then he concentrated on the resulting pleasure.

For example, loneliness was the pain. The need for companionship would cause action. Companionship was the pleasure. The need for companionship would cause a person to act.

What did Maslow do with his findings?

Abraham Maslow took all the positive elements that would give a person pleasure. He then arranged them into what he considered a hierarchy of importance. For example, the need for food was more important than mankind's need for fame.

Mankind's need for fame was more important than the need to discover one's purpose in life, and so on.

He grouped related pleasures into categories and then arranged the categories into what he considered to be their order of importance. The resulting hierarchy of categories is:

1 SURVIVAL needs: the pleasures that produce action in order to avoid pain are:
Food
Drink
Shelter

2 SAFETY needs: the pleasures that produce action in order to avoid pain are:
Feeling secure
Predictable environment
Rules
Structure
No economic anxiety
No psychological anxiety

3 LOVE and BELONGING needs: the pleasures that produce action in order to avoid pain are:
Connection with other people
Affection
Part of a family
Part of a group
Part of society

4 ESTEEM needs: the pleasures that produce action in order to avoid pain are:

Self-confidence
Recognition
Fame
Being appreciated
Being respected

5 SELF ACTUALISATION needs: the pleasures that produce action in order to avoid pain are:
Achieving one's potential
Accomplishing what one wants in life
Discovering one's purpose in life
Attaining things that one considers important

Give me an example of minor events

As an example of using minor events, first consider the major event.
For example, take the major event of the story as 'Person needs to fight the enemy to save the tribe'.

- Dragon is about to terrorise the village
- Village weakling **feels insignificant** (pain) and **wants fame** (pleasure)
- The **need for fame** (need) produces action
- Village weakling offers to save the village folk
- Weakling faces dragon
- Weakling almost killed
- Weakling sees cliff edge
- Weakling gets dragon to follow him towards the cliff edge
- Weakling jumps aside and dragon falls over cliff

- Villagers saved, weakling becomes a hero (*the need for fame caused the action*).

Conclusion

Just as the five major problems start the action in your story, so the five minor problems continue the action. They hold your audience's interest and maintain their attention. If you want your story to be longer, you just add more minor problems.

Chapter 4

MINOR PLOTS: emotions cause action

In the previous chapter, you learned that needs/drives/desires (I will call these 'needs' from now on) make people act. The stimulus for most needs is internal.

In this chapter, you will learn about emotions. Emotions also cause people to act. The stimulus for most emotions is external.

Knowing needs and emotions helps you to get your main character into action and your story to show movement. Needs and emotions cause a character to make decisions. Choices and decisions are a great way to engage your audience's attention.

Emotions result in action

When you are restrained, you become angry, you fight. When someone dies, you become sad, you cry. Emotions cause action.

Both needs and emotions result in action. Knowing their causes provides the storyteller with numerous ideas for action scenes.

Action is important because it is the only way that the audience knows if the character is determined to change events. Your audience wants to be convinced that your character is committed to the cause. Action is best way to illustrate this commitment.

What is the purpose of emotion?

Emotions evolved in order to protect you. They enable you to act quickly when faced with events that may affect your survival. You act, you survive. The emotions make the assessments, make the decisions and produce actions. You live. The emotions take over. They direct your thoughts, your words, your actions. The emotions are spontaneous and were given to mankind to help the species to survive.

The changes in your body happen so quickly that you may not be aware of them. Facial expressions, voice, heartbeat and body posture all change automatically. The reaction is different for each emotion.

Some reactions are so spontaneous that they appear more innate than learned. Psychologists have pondered the basis of emotions over the centuries.

Discovering the major emotions inspired Charles Darwin to conduct research for his book called *The Expression of Emotions in Man and Animals*. He noticed that some emotions had recognisable facial expressions. Darwin wanted to know which facial expressions were recognised by all human beings.

He had an actor portray facial emotions and hired a photographer to capture the result. He then gave the photographs to various scholars and missionaries and asked them to report their findings from different parts of the world – Australia, New Zealand, Malaysia, Borneo, India, Ceylon and Papua New Guinea. Report after report showed that there were seven facial expressions that were universal. All nations understood the emotion that the face was expressing.

Paul Ekman in his book *Emotions Revealed – Understanding Faces and Feelings*, conducted a similar experiment in the 1950s. He showed photographs of facial expressions to different cultures – in Chile, Argentina, Brazil, Japan, Papua New Guinea and the United States. Again, the findings were the same. There were seven facial expressions that all cultures recognised which are associated with a specific emotion.

The seven emotions they identified are:
fear; disgust; anger; sadness; surprise; contempt, and joy.

Why are these seven emotions important to survival?

1 Fear

Fear alerts you to danger. Danger can be a loud noise or a sudden movement.

Fear prepares you to flee if the threat is too great and enables you to avoid battle and possible death. It can cause you to freeze if you think this will reduce the likelihood of you being seen. It can also signal to the aggressor that you are yielding and hence are not a threat. On the other hand, it can motivate you to fight if you are confident that you can overcome the aggressor.

Our facial expression of fear can help the species survive by notifying others that there is danger nearby. It can also be a plea for help to overcome an aggressor.

2 Disgust

Disgust protects the body from anything that could be harmful or contaminating, and so protects your health. The function of disgust is to remove you from anything that is revolting. Revulsion towards the physical signs of suffering and disease help you to avoid contagious diseases. Disgust is targeted at objects not people.

3 Anger

Anger prepares mankind for attack. It can communicate to an aggressor the willingness but not the intent to fight. This show of strength can have survival advantages. Anger can also provide the energy to motivate action and deal with the threat.

On a social level, your anger can warn others that you are a threat. It is quicker for others to see what emotion you are signalling rather than you having to tell them. Your angry facial expression can inform others that their actions are not acceptable. This prevents unnecessary confrontation. Anger is aroused most vigorously when a person stops you from reaching your intended goal.

4 Sadness

Sadness or grief results from loss. It is a sense of helplessness. The purpose of sadness is to draw attention to your need for help. It indicates your intention to reach out and ask for the comfort of others in the group. Tears put a person in a state of confusion and paralysis. They are literally unable to see where they are going. Sadness encourages a person to retreat from social life. This prevents them from damaging their social standing or being rejected by their social group.

A person may not express their sadness until they are in a group that understands their sorrow and shares their loss. The act of telling others of their grief and experiencing their consoling actions helps reduce the sadness. Culture influences the expression of sorrow. Some societies do not encourage visible expression while others wholeheartedly encourage it.

Sadness has a positive effect on society. Members feel good when they comfort others and see how they have reduced their misery.

5 Surprise

Surprise is that moment before a person understands what is happening. It alerts the body's defence mechanisms to be on stand-by. It focuses the person's attention on the event of the moment. It quickly changes to another emotion after an evaluation of the threat level (*e.g. non-threatening = joy, threatening = anger*). The person responds to the event accordingly.

6 Contempt

Contempt relates to people, not things ('things' are the concern of disgust). It is the feeling of superiority over others who do not obey social norms. Experiencing the feeling of approval is sufficient to ensure most people in society obey the rules and that the rules are obeyed.

7 Joy

Joy causes a person to do things that are good for them and ensures the survival of the species (eat, drink and have sex).

In a social setting, joy is a powerful bonding emotion. It is experienced when loved ones meet. People feel understood and appreciated. The sound of laughter is itself a sign of being a member of the group. It indicates that the person wants to be one with their fellows, has no harmful intentions towards them and agrees to adopt their social customs.

Which emotional events will cause your character to act?

1 FEAR

Fear is the response to an external stimulus that motivates a person to be ready for action. It is a motivator to avoid pain. You are born with a sense of fear. The emotional events that will trigger action from your character are:

*threat of harm – physical, psychological, external, internal
*loud noises
*sudden changes and movement
*something hurtling through space quickly that will hurt them if they do not move
*the sudden loss of support that will result in their falling through space
*being in a high place where a false step might lead to a fall
*separation from loved ones
*snakes and spiders

*if the person threatening them seems to be more powerful
*inability to cope with a threat.

2 DISGUST

Disgust is a reaction to anything that could harm our bodies and cause death.
The emotional events that will trigger action from your character are:

*something inedible – rotten food, faeces
*illness
*bitter taste in the mouth
*associations that have the look and smell of something inedible
*dirty objects
*superstitions about foods
*bodily products – faeces, vomit, urine, mucus, blood
*gore
*dead bodies
*repulsive animals
*wounds
*deformity
*anything contaminating.

3 ANGER

Anger is generally the result of an appraisal of a situation. It involves a threatening situation or the breaking of social rules. The emotional events that will trigger action from your character are:

*threatening provocation
*when someone is trying to hurt them physically
*deliberate interference with what they are determined to do
*personal slight – denigrating their appearance or their performance
*when someone is trying to hurt them psychologically
*demeaning offence
*being unfairly treated
*when someone else is to blame
*frustration
*threatening encounters
*being rejected by a loved one.

4 SADNESS

Sadness is an emotion that results from loss. The emotional events that will that will trigger action from your character are:

*feeling that they have no control over the loss
*feeling the loss is not their fault
*feeling the loss is irrevocable
*experiencing the loss of someone close
*experiencing the loss of members of a social group
*experiencing rejection by a friend or lover
*feeling the loss of self-esteem resulting from failure to reach a goal
*experiencing the loss of admiration or praise from a superior
*the loss of health, body part, body function.
*when an infant is separated from the parent
*the loss of a treasured object.

5 SURPRISE

Surprise is a response to a novel or unexpected stimulus. As soon as the questioning is completed, the surprise emotion disappears, and an appropriate emotion follows. The emotional events that will trigger action from your character are:

*novelty
*confusion
*unfamiliarity
*unexpectedness
*sudden event
*incongruity.

6 CONTEMPT

Contempt has similarities to disgust but is directed at people and expresses distaste for the immoral acts of others. The emotional events that will trigger action from your character are:

*revulsion of moral violations
*actions of others that they find deplorable
*greed of others
*corruption
*dishonest acts
*people who do not conform to social rules
*people who are below their social level.

7 JOY

Joy is considered a positive emotion. It is associated with reward or pleasure. The emotional events that will trigger action from your character are:

*pleasurable social encounters
*sensory pleasure – sight, sound, taste, touch, smell
*reunion with loved ones
*love
*trust
*play
*success in learning or skill development
*sex
*hearing something funny or amusing.

Have emotions evolved?

The triggers of the common emotions still exist but there have been some modifications. The causes of these emotions have been transferred to other objects. For example, the terror of the spear has been replaced by the gun. The threat of a fierce lion has been replaced by the attack of a mugger.

Learning
You can learn to have an emotional reaction. Children can be taught to fear germs. Adults can learn which political parties are good or bad. You can associate neutral objects with previous good or bad experiences.

Social
Social situations have evolved. Etiquette and social norms put restrictions on mankind's behaviour. Threats are more mental

than physical. Loss of job is regarded as more frightening than the scourge of an epidemic or plague.

Memory
Recalling an emotional event can trigger reactions. Hearing words that recall events of the past can trigger emotional reactions. As the world evolves and our experiences widen, the circumstances that have emotional associations will increase.

Summary
Emotions still have the same purpose – to help you survive. They cause your characters to act. They help your characters to assess and interact with an ever-changing environment. Emotions initiate action.

Chapter 5

EMPATHY: ensures audience involvement

In the last chapter you learned more about emotions and how they resulted in action. In this chapter, you will meet empathy and discover why it is related to emotions. You will learn how empathy can involve your audience. Empathy is another tool for getting your audience's attention and maintaining their interest.

What is empathy?

Empathy is the capacity to identify with what another person is thinking and feeling. As a result, you react with a similar emotional state. You mentally adopt the feelings of the character and mentally act the same way as the character. You leave reality. You experience the events of fantasy.

If I see, do I react?

Psychologists have found that parts of your brain are activated when you observe someone performing an action. Your brain simulates the action and you mentally experience what you see.

In 1996, Giacomo Rizzolatti and his team at the University of Parma in Italy attached electrodes to a monkey's brain. They wanted to find out which neurons in the brain were activated when the monkey grasped an object. They discovered that when a monkey grasped an object, neurons fired in specific sectors of the brain.

Then, during a break, one of the researchers picked up a knife. Fellow researchers noticed something extraordinary happened on the monitor. Neurons in the monkey's brain fired, which were the same neurons that had fired earlier when the monkey itself grasped an object.

Their accidental finding was the first clue to the existence of what scientists now call 'mirror neurons'. The monkey's neurons fired as if it had made the same movement itself. The monkey was showing empathy, empathy being the stimulation of a person's brain caused by watching the actions of another.

When humans watch the action of others, the sectors of the brain that are stimulated are the same sectors that are activated when they perform the action themselves.

Further research hypothesized that not only actions but also sensations and emotions displayed by others can cause empathy and be understood. This is caused by the 'mirror neurons' in the brain. This theory has now been established and forms the basis of why stories, theatre and movies cause an emotional reaction in you. In other words, empathy.

If I hear, do I empathise?

Not only do you experience the actions of others when you see them, you also experience them when you hear a description of their actions.

Words can produce empathy.

You can listen to the actions of your characters and feel what they are feeling. Part of your brain is sensitive to words. Words can suspend reality and allow you to enter a fantasy world. You become less conscious of yourself and you blur the distinction between reality and fantasy.

As a storyteller, you have a wonderful gift. You can describe a scene and your audience will experience the same feelings as your character. You can take your audience from the here and now and transport them into your world of fantasy.

Empathy and brain sectors

Empathy is the capacity to recognise and identify with what another person is thinking and feeling. You then react with a comparable emotional state. Watching another person perform an action stimulates the same parts of the brain as if you were doing the action yourself. One of those brain regions is the amygdala – the seat of the emotions.

Another brain region that is stimulated is the inferior frontal gyrus (IFG). The IFG is involved with the processing of language. It helps us understand words, so not only visual stimuli but also words cause empathy.

Yet another brain region that is activated is the posterior superior temporal sulcus (pSTS). This is an area of the brain that enables the comprehension of text and verbal processing. It understands the relationship between plot, character and writing style. Also, pSTS blurs the distinction between reality and fantasy. You are temporarily transported to the world of the author, filmmaker or storyteller.

Empathy helps you to appreciate the emotions of another and experience part of their life.

Conclusion

Images of your character in action cause your audience to participate in the story. Not only images but also words can create the same experience in the minds of your readers. Empathy is a wonderful way of engaging your readers' attention and interest.

Chapter 6

CHARACTERS: behaviour preceded titles

In this chapter, you will meet the 'characters' behind the actions. While behaviour can differ, there are groups of behaviours that are similar, so much so that one could give a name to a familiar group of behaviours. The name given to an identifiable collection of behaviours is 'archetype'. Specific archetypes have a name.

Examples of related behaviours and their archetype

For example, the behaviours of teaching, training, lecturing, tutoring, counselling and instructing are all similar. It is an identifiable collection of behaviours. The ancients called characters that exhibited this pattern the archetype 'Mentor'. Anyone who performed this function was regarded as a 'mentor'. When you describe a character as a mentor, your audience automatically assumes that you are referring to a person who teaches or advises another. Archetype refers to a pattern of behaviour rather than a character.

How many archetypes are there?

There were seven groups of behaviour that the ancients saw frequently. Certain individuals exemplified a specific group of behaviours. Ancients named that group of behaviours after the individual. The individual personified the collection of behaviours. The seven archetype characters are:

1 Mother
2 Father
3 Child
4 Hero
5 Villain
6 Mentor
7 Trickster

They are so common to all cultures that each culture gave them alternative names. The optional titles are:

1 Mother – Queen, Ruler
2 Father – King, Ruler
3 Child – Innocent, Youth
4 Hero
5 Villain
6 Mentor – Wise Old Man, Crone
7 Trickster – Jester, Fool

Archetype Mother: behaviour patterns

The actions of the Archetype Mother included feeding the child, helping the partner and making garments for the family. She would also gently rebuke the child if there was the possibility of it harming itself. She was loving but firm. She was caring but watchful. Any character who shows these qualities of 'caring' are included in the Archetype Mother. These would include the nurse, doctor and foster mother.

Archetype Father: behaviour patterns

The male was responsible for protecting his family. If the family needed food, he would hunt. He would show his child the skills of the hunter, take them on adventures, prepare them for life outside the family. Any character showing these behaviours was called the Archetype Father. As society developed, the role of the father changed. Hunters became farmers. Families became extended families and clans. The responsibility of the father grew, and his role became more authoritarian. He became a ruler, a king. The Archetype Father included the father of a nation, where the nation should be interpreted as a larger family.

Archetype Child: behaviour patterns

The child would be watching, learning, experimenting. It would enjoy new experiences, be alert to excitement and unaware of danger. Every child exhibited the same behaviour pattern. Every day, every month, the same pattern. Eventually these behaviour patterns were burned into mankind's psyche. They became an archetype, the archetype called Child. Anyone having similar traits was classed as the Archetype Child.

Archetype Hero: behaviour patterns

The hero was concerned about the safety of the group. The hero would accept responsibility for the welfare of the tribe and would ensure their safety. It could be fighting the dragon or finding new territory. There would always be an element of danger involved. Eventually, the hero would emerge victorious. He would return to the group and ensure they all prospered.

This frequent behaviour pattern was burned into mankind's psyche. The hero's actions became an archetype. Anyone exhibiting similar behaviour was classed as the Archetype Hero.

Archetype Villain: behaviour patterns

Early mankind would have seen a predator on the prowl, or the enemy warrior poised for attack. The experience of being hunted was burned into mankind's psyche. The behaviour of the aggressor or enemy became the archetype called Villain. Everyone knew what you meant by this term. It was a universal concept.

If the villain initiated the action, the hero would react. If the hero initiated the action, the villain would react. The scenario was familiar to all and the concept is alive today. The presence of the Archetype Villain means conflict for the Archetype Hero.

Archetype Mentor: behaviour patterns

The purpose of the mentor is to help the Hero succeed. The mentor's role was positive. The mentor would prepare the hero for the tasks ahead. The mentor would give the hero the necessary physical equipment, training, and skills required for success. It was up to the hero, however, to use these advantages to succeed. The mentor was not involved in any confrontations. Any person, animal or circumstance that prepared the hero to succeed was called the Archetype Mentor.

Archetype Trickster: behaviour patterns

The trickster's task was to protect the hero from danger *(as distinct from the Archetype Mentor whose task was to prepare the hero to face danger)*. The trickster could be Fate which inspired the hero to move, saving him from the falling boulder. It could be a court jester who intervened just in time to save the hero from a disastrous marriage. Any character whose pattern of actions helped the hero avoid misfortune was given the name Archetype Trickster.

Conclusion

Archetypes are patterns of behaviour that can be attributed to a specific person. Certain patterns of behaviour became fixed in man's psyche. The archetype was named after the specific person who demonstrated that pattern of behaviour. You met seven archetypes in this chapter: *Mother, Father, Child, Hero, Villain, Mentor and Trickster*.

When you use archetypes in your stories, they should relate to the actions of the character. You have seen that certain groups of actions (archetypes) are fixed in the mind of humanity. Knowing these archetypes gives you a quick way to identify your character and events that your audience can recognise.

Chapter 7

CONTEXT: time and place, when and where

'Once upon a time, in a place far away . . .'
'He got the call around nine pm. It had been a long night in the city . . .'
'Daylight was fading, and the moon struggled above the crest of the mountain . . .'

Why do most stories start with a time and a place? From tales of old to modern-day novels, the storyteller feels compelled to inform their audience of when and where the action took place.

Why does mankind feel more comfortable when they know time and place?

Professor Susan Engel, a child psychologist, may provide the answer. Her research asked young children about their daily routines. The child instinctively spoke about time and place. "At bedtime (time) I go to my room (place) and put on my pyjamas . . ." or "In the morning (time) I get out of bed (place) and put on my top . . ." Professor Engel called these descriptions 'scripts'. The script always contained a reference to a time and a place.

What upsets a child when they have learned a routine?

Professor Engel noted something else. If the parent changed the child's established routine, the child would protest. The child would state that there was something wrong. Engel talks of the child who went to the park every Wednesday by a certain route. One day the mother changed the route. The child noticed immediately that familiar places had changed and tried to correct her.

What has logic got to do with you?

Engel's findings are of great importance to the storyteller. The child was fully aware of any deviation from what they were expecting. If there was any variation in the routine, the child would immediately notice and try to halt proceedings. Subconsciously, the child was aware of the time and place of the event and also what experience to expect.

For you as a storyteller, this observation is important. Once you establish the story's time and location, everything thereafter must correspond with that setting. Clothing, buildings, décor must all reinforce the era that you have chosen.

Consistency is important because if something is not appropriate, your audience will pause. They will analyse, they will think. They will come out of their imagination zone. They will leave your world of story and enter their world of logic. You have lost the attention of your audience.

What has credibility got to do with this?

For you as a storyteller, you must respect the mindset your audience. Once you betray them by taking them down an unexpected route, they will question your sincerity.

Your audience has inherited certain mental templates. You saw in previous chapters that certain structures, characters and actions are built into mankind's psyche. Making use of those elements gives pleasure to your audience. When you deviate from these time-honoured traditions, you run the risk of alienating your audience and lowering your storytelling status.

What is one definition of 'story'?

When you tell a story, you are describing a completed action. The event has happened. It is not here. It is not now. It takes place in another place and at another time.

You are also asking your audience to step into the unknown. You want them to leave their safe world and enter your world of fantasy. They want to know where they are going. They want an indication of what to expect. Giving the time and place helps them to quickly identify what they might encounter. The element of uncertainty disappears, and the stage is set for entertainment.

The same reasoning applies to stories that are set in the future. Future events need the same indication of time and place. Without some clues, your audience will be more concerned with their own thoughts and guesses rather than the story that you are telling.

Conclusion

Children have an innate need to relate events to a time and a place. A story is about another time and another place Your audience feels more comfortable when they know where they are going and what to expect. Eliminating possible questions that might arise in your audience's minds helps them to participate and enjoy their stay in your fantasy world.

Chapter 8

DESCRIPTIONS: describe the event and let your characters react

Your choice of words, the tense of the verbs and the descriptions of events have an impact on your tale. Words and their use have evolved just as mankind has evolved. In this chapter you will discover the importance of describing events and the way your character reacts. Reactions are a great way to get your audience's attention. They just have to know what the character did next.

EXPERIENCES

Pain and pleasure

Early mankind was preoccupied with survival. Their senses were alert. They saw, they heard, they smelled, they tasted, they touched. Each sensation contributed to a memory. Each experience was analysed. Was the result pain or was the result pleasure? Pain and pleasure became the criteria by which events were measured. Events were emotional experiences. Crude at first, just pain and pleasure.

Emotions

These emotional reactions were graded as time went on. Some fruits were good, others bad and some in between. Similarly, there were animals that were fierce while others could be domesticated. Mankind was building a bank of memories based on emotional reactions. The environment was assessed by the degree of pleasure or pain it triggered. For thousands of years, mankind thought in terms of emotions.

As a writer and a storyteller, you need to be aware of emotions and emotional reactions. These have always been at the heart of every experience that mankind has endured.

MEMORY

Five senses

Early mankind had no words. Experiences were catalogued according to their pain-pleasure value. Life was emotional, and their sense of sight, sound, smell, taste and touch was the input that determined the output. If you input the sight of danger, the output would be the emotional reaction of fear. Input the sound of a loved one and the output would be the emotional reaction of joy.

As storytellers, you need to be conscious that the senses precede the emotional reaction. Use your senses to describe the scene, then let your characters experience the emotional reaction.

Bigger brain

Evolution added to mankind's brain. The brain now possessed the cerebral cortex. It was an addition. It was not a replacement. All the feelings and sensations that man previously experienced were still dominant. This new element to the brain enabled mankind to speak. He was also able to recall. Man was able to talk about incidents in the past. He was becoming a storyteller.

Man could describe his experiences to others. Initial descriptions were graphic. They concerned life-or-death situations. They involved the senses. They described what he saw, smelled, heard, tasted and touched. They revealed his reaction and what he felt.

As a storyteller, you need to be conscious that mankind has always had experiences that started with the senses. Then there was an emotional reaction. Your story should reflect the emotional reaction and the resulting behaviour.

Societies

As tribes got bigger, they became societies, large groups of people each having their own goals and ambitions. The physical conflict with Nature took a step back. The mental conflict with other human beings gained dominance. The need arose for laws to inhibit bad behaviour and laws to encourage good behaviour. Humans became the new predator. The laws of Nature were replaced by civil and criminal codes.

Emotions finely tuned

As societies developed, stories revolved around experiences that involved humans rather than animals. The emotions of the previous thousands of years were still dominant. Pain or pleasure, with all the degrees in between, was experienced. Anger could be merely annoyed or incredibly furious. Happy could be pleased or ecstatic. The stories created in later societies reflected their emotions and related more to people than to survival in the wild.

Actions and the five senses

The early societies loved stories with action. The confrontation was between man and Nature. Later, territorial disputes, empire building and the thirst for power fuelled the action. Warriors would return from battle and recall events to an eager listener. The stories would give graphic details of sounds, sights and action. Each blow of the sword would have had an accompanying emotion. They would describe the pain of the victim, the pleasure of the victor. Mankind now had the memory and the language to recall these events and the character's reactions.

As a storyteller, you should note that words were used to describe what their senses experienced and what their emotions felt. The event was described and the character's reactions followed.

IMAGINATION

Approximately 20,000 years ago, evolution gave mankind another gift. The brain developed the capacity to imagine. Mankind possessed imagination. Previously, man was able to recall only past events. The event had to have happened. It needed a beginning, a middle and an end. The storyteller's task was to remember the episode and then arrange the events in sequence. The tales were all in the past. They were real and they happened.

With the gift of imagination, man could leave the here and now and travel backward or forward in time. No other creature is able to do this. Mankind has this unique gift.

Freedom of movement

While early mankind was bound by the laws of Nature, people in early societies were limited by the laws of society. Today you can create your own reality. You are free of limitations. You have the gift of imagination. Your creatures can have any hue, their actions can defy gravity and you can be the mastermind of any plot. Your creativity is limited only by your imagination. And your imagination is unlimited. You can truly create your own universe. You can invite your audience to share your world.

Past or future

Your imagined world can be in the past or it can be in the future. If you have chosen a future scenario (e.g. *Star Wars*), the tale must still have a beginning, middle and end. The event must be completed. It is a story. The here and now may change but your audience still wants to know the story's climax and resolution. They want to know how it ends.

Credibility

With great power comes responsibility. Once you have established your time frame, you must remain faithful to it.

Your characters, your props and your scenes must all confirm your new world. If a sword is magical, then it must work wonders and the scenes must show this. If your character is superhuman, then the action must demonstrate this.

Your audience has the imagination and the capacity to share your imaginary world. They can accept the transcendence of time and the transformation of objects. But once in your world, they need consistency. If you violate this trust, you create confusion. When an audience is confused, they leave your world. They lose interest. You have lost their attention.

As a storyteller, once you create your imaginary world you must ensure that characters, objects and events are commensurate.

SUMMARY

From early times to the present day, mankind has experienced the environment and society in terms of pain or pleasure. Emotions and feelings guided his survival. Pain meant avoid. Pleasure meant approach.

Man's five senses were always active. When mankind had the power of speech, he could articulate what he saw, heard, touched. He had the words to clarify his emotions and how he felt. He could express verbally what he thought. Mankind had the power to describe an event and the ability to articulate a reaction.

As a storyteller, you have the power of speech and writing. Your audience has inherited the power to imagine scenarios that you describe in words, to feel the emotional reactions of your characters and to experience the here and now of your environment.

The mind of mankind has evolved. Your audience has been part of this transition. Use evolution's gifts of the five senses, emotions, words and imagination to make your story spectacular.

Chapter 9

PUTTING IT ALL TOGETHER

What should I write about? (Theme, topic/subject)

Theme

Theme summarises what the author wants to say about life, about being human. Theme transcends racial, cultural and religious connotations. It is a universal statement that everyone can relate to.

Theme can be a concept *e.g. Love.*
Theme can be an affirmation *e.g. Love conquers all.*
Theme can be a supposition, 'x leads to y'. *e.g. Love leads to murder.*

Your story is intended to prove your theme.

Topic/subject

Any of the following list can trigger an idea for your story:
- Printed material – newspaper articles, magazines, books
- Media – TV, radio, film
- Social media – Facebook comments, Instagram
- Conversations – at home, work, on the bus
- Events – something that happened to you or to others
- Characters – people you have met, their opinions, attitudes, beliefs

- What if? – take any situation and ask the question.

You are looking for an idea that you feel strongly about. You believe that 'this' is the way things should be. You are convinced you are right, and you want the world to agree with you.

Once you have your idea, you are ready to assemble your story.

What pattern should my story take? (Structure)

Down–struggle–up

You saw in a previous chapter that Nature's pattern is down–struggle–up. The flower blooms, it dies, it rises again. You saw how there was a struggle before it rose again. There was conflict. Then there was success and finally a resolution.

Knowing the basic pattern of your story gives you confidence to add, remove and change the details.

What does my audience need to know immediately? (Context)

A story, by its very nature, takes the listener from the here and now to a different place and a different time. Your audience needs these coordinates to better appreciate the details of your story. They need to know the context. The sooner you indicate your story's time and place, the sooner your audience can enter your imaginary world.

Which people should I include? (Characters)

As soon as language evolved, the first stories were always about people. Initially, the storyteller was the hero of the event. Events were man against animals and Nature. As society developed, the struggles involved man against man. The traits of a person took precedence. Use the knowledge from the Terminology section to describe your good and your bad characters.

Why does my character want to get involved? (Motivation)

Characters do not act unless they want to avoid pain or gain pleasure. This is called motivation. Needs are the obvious source of motivation as they imply pain and label the gain. Needs are concerned with the person and their personal development. They are initiated internally.

Emotions are another source of motivation They can move a person to action. They involve people. They can cause action or be the result of another's action. They are initiated externally.

What is at the heart of a story? (Conflict)

Life is a struggle and stories are about life, so the heart of a story is struggle. From the beginning of time, the story has been about people and their struggles. Primitive man fought animals. Your ancestors battled against invaders. The audience enjoyed the suspense of the confrontation – what options were available, what decision was made? Choices and decisions arouse curiosity and curiosity gets the audience's attention. People, struggle, choices and decisions are basic to every good story.

One event with conflict can create a short story. For longer stories, there needs to be a succession of events. One event must cause the next. There has to be a causal connection between events. The last big conflict is often called the climax. It precedes the ending or resolution.

What happens when the conflict ends? (Resolution)

Psychologists found that children did not feel a story was complete until there were two elements. These were a climax and a resolution. University students confirmed this finding when tested. There has to be some description of a horrible conflict, worse than any yet described. This should be followed by a section answering all the questions that have been raised.

Summary

Stories leave the here and now and take the listener to an imaginary world. This world is another time and another place. It has a different context. Stories have always involved people. There were good people and there were bad people. Each had their own character traits. The antagonist forced the protagonist to struggle. Struggle meant choices and decisions. Audiences enjoyed guessing which decision would be made. They enjoyed hearing the resulting consequences. Eventually the story would end when all the story's questions were answered.

Incorporate these time-honoured elements into your story and your story will be a success.

TERMINOLOGY

I include this section to explain terms that you might meet if you do further research. The intention is to give definitions that several authorities agree upon.

Confusion can arise when the same term is used in different contexts. Some authors use different terms interchangeably. Others are more specific in their definitions. Sometimes one book will give a completely different explanation to another.

In an effort to find a definition that most authors agree upon, I include the findings of my research. I hope these help.

Chapter 10

TERMINOLOGY:

Verse, Prose, Narrative, Story, Plot, Theme, Premise

Verse
Verse is any writing that is arranged with a metrical rhythm and usually rhymes.

It has meter, rhyme and rhythm. It follows some type of pattern.

Prose
Prose is anything that is not verse. It has no meter, no rhyme and no rhythm.

Prose uses ordinary language and uses regular grammatical conventions.

It includes fiction and non-fiction.

Narrative
Narrative is a sub-category of prose. There are other types of prose e.g. fictional prose, heroic prose, etc. In this book you will focus on narrative prose (also called 'narrative') which concentrates on stories.

There is confusion about the definition of 'narrative' because narrative and story are used interchangeably as are narrative, story and plot. Also, narrative is often used to describe something that tells a story.

Narrative is:
the selection of events that the writer wants to include in the story
and
the order in which to present them
and
all the techniques that impact on how the story is told (tone, frame, etc).

Narrative is the framework for the story rather than the story itself. It is the what, the who and the how of a given sequence of events.

Narrative is the way you deliver a story using the events you have selected in the order that you present them. If you change the order of events you change the narrative – not the story.

Two writers can describe the same set of events. If the order of those same events is changed, you will meet two different narratives. For example, the events of the same soccer match would be arranged in a different order by Team A compared with Team B's account. They are the same event, but they have different narratives. The order of events would be different. You would have two narratives but only one story.

Narrative Structure
1 Inciting incident
This is the event that starts the protagonist's predicament and initiates the conflicts.

2 Complications

The obstacles that the protagonist faces. They make the final goal difficult to reach.

3 Crisis

This can be an event that must be faced to avoid a disastrous outcome. It can be a change in fortunes. It can be a point where the story takes a new direction.

4 Climax

This is the moment when the protagonist will succeed or fail. The hero usually succeeds. The conflict is resolved. The goal is reached.

5 Resolution/denouement

Any issues that have not been resolved are now resolved. The action ends.

Story

Story is a sub category of narrative.

There are two main types of story:

1 Chronological story

This is a series of events that are connected by temporal conjunctions.

Temporal conjunctions are 'then', 'and then', 'next'.

The events are arranged in time sequence, e.g. biographies, memoirs.

2 Plot story

This is a series of events that are connected by causal conjunctions.

Causal conjunctions are 'because', 'as a result'.

Each event causes the next event, which causes the next event, etc.

(*Character story* – this story concentrates on the character's development rather than on the plot or the actual events.)

Plot

Plot is an integral part of the 'Plot story'.

It is a literary term used to describe the events that make up a story.

Plot is what happens during each event and how each event is connected. It indicates how one event causes the next. There is a causal connection. There is a chain of causes and effect. The choices considered and the decisions made by the protagonist have repercussions.

The events are deliberately arranged so as to highlight the dramatic, thematic and emotional significance to the story. The intensity of the conflict increases as the story progresses.

A 'story' is the combination of individual events while 'plot' is what happens during each individual event.

Theme

Theme is the idea, the message or the moral of the story.

It is what the story is about. Your story should prove your theme.

The writer has something to say about the condition of the world and wants others to come to see the world in the same way. It is the writer's opinion about a topic. It is the message that the writer wants the audience to discover.

Theme is the critical belief about life that the author is trying to convey. This belief should transcend cultural barriers and be universal in nature. When a theme is universal, it touches on human experience, regardless of race or language.

Some writers see 'theme' as being a one-word subject or topic, e.g. *love*.
Other writers define 'theme' using a sentence, e.g. *love conquers all*.

Theme is often formulated before you start writing.

Premise
Premise should not be confused with 'theme'.
Premise is a storyline that can be encapsulated in one or two sentences.
It indicates what the story is about. It highlights the dramatic situation at the heart of the story.

A premise is the plot using one or two sentences. A story premise is most useful when it names:
- a specific character
- a specific problem
- a specific goal.

A premise is not an abstract idea. It describes action, particularly action that causes problems for someone.

A premise is often formulated after you have thought about your story's content.

Chapter 11

TERMINOLOGY:
Genres

A genre is a category of composition. A specific genre has similarities in the subject matter, style and form. Genres fulfil the audience's expectations. Audiences buy certain books because they have enjoyed similar stories in the past.

Literary genre

The different types of literary genre include:

Classic:
Classic fiction is the type of work that has been generally accepted for educational purposes. Works that fit into this category would be the books you studied in secondary school and university literature classes.

Crime:
This genre focuses on the crime itself. It may discuss how the criminal gets caught or why the crime was committed in the first place.

Drama:
These are typically stories that are created through the use of prose, verse or scenes. Movies and plays fit into this genre, as do certain books where the conflict and emotion are expressed in dialogue and action.

Fable:

These stories offer readers certain truths or opinions in a supernatural way. In many fables, it is animals who speak or take on human characteristics.

Fairy tale:

This genre originally received its name because it told stories about fairies. Now any story about a magical land or creatures will typically qualify as being part of this category.

Fan fiction:

This is a relatively new genre. It is a story that is written by a fan but incorporates characters, scenes and locations that were originally created by someone else.

Fantasy:

This type of work will include settings that occur somewhere else in the universe. Characters may seem strange but that's because this category invites a complete suspension of reality.

Graphic fiction:

This is the category for comic books and graphic novels.

Historical:

This genre offers readers events and fictional characters that occur within a historical setting. Sometimes real people are included to interact with the fictional characters to create an extra sense of realism.

Horror:

The goal of this type of story is to create feelings of fear and dread. Although some might think of this genre as being full of 'blood and gore', anything that happens to create these negative feelings can qualify as horror.

Humour:
This genre is designed to entertain but good humour will also have an underlying thought or concept.

Mystery:
This genre is often associated with crime, usually murder, but it doesn't have to be. It includes any story that involves the unravelling of secrets.

Mythology:
This type of story involves the traditional narratives that have become part of a culture over different eras. These may be based on human events, natural phenomena, or even have religious significance. Many of the images used in this genre will have multiple meanings and are open to interpretation by the reader.

Realism:
These are stories that are true to life. Sometimes they may be inspired by real events.

Science fiction:
This genre examines the past, current and future impact of science on our society. It may also do this from an alien perspective.

Suspense:
This genre puts the main character in a dangerous situation. The story follows the character as they attempt to escape.

Westerns:
This genre takes place in the Old West of the United States, usually taking place in the late 1800s or early 1900s. The stories may include romance, suspense and realism at various levels.

NON-FICTION stories

Non-fiction stories also have different types of genres: biographies; essays; personal narratives; textbooks; self-help books, and journalism are different forms of non-fiction writing.

Summary

The different genres are designed to distinguish what a work is and what a reader can expect. It makes it easier for the writer to connect to the reader in a meaningful way.

Chapter 12

TERMINOLOGY:
Character Roles, Characterisation

In previous chapters, you met characters under the guise of 'archetypes'. Archetypes are patterns of behaviour shared by similar characters; they are not the character themselves. Over time, the definition of 'character' and its explanation has become more and more detailed. In this chapter you will meet the many roles that a character can play in a story.

What are the roles that a character can play?

In today's literature, you will see 'character' defined as any person, animal, inanimate object, figure or nature. The roles that the character can play are often explained in terms of the plot. The following are the most common characters in terms of plot.

Protagonist
This is the main character who is responsible for the action in the plot.

Antagonist
This is the character who creates obstacles for the protagonist.

Dynamic character or Developing character
This person changes during the story. The change can be physical or it can be mental.

Static character

This character remains the same throughout the story. There is no change in their outlook or motivation. They may have many character traits, but these do not change.

Round character

This character is well developed and is complex. They have depth and often make surprising choices. They react to each situation.

Flat character

The person does not change throughout the story. Unlike the static character who has many traits, the flat character has just a few, usually only one.

Major character (also called the Protagonist)

This character is at the centre of the plot.

Minor character

This character complements the major character and helps to move the plot forward.

Stock character

This character has the same role regardless of the topic of the story. They are one-dimensional and their behaviour is predictable.

Anti-hero (Antagonist)

The character is usually the antagonist. They do not have admirable qualities. They create obstacles for the protagonist. They often have their own evil agenda.

Foil
This is any character who helps to emphasise the protagonist's character and qualities.

Symbolic character
This is any character who represents some aspect of society, such as logic or cruelty.

Confidant
This character is someone in whom the main character/protagonist will confide. The confidant reveals the main character's thoughts. It can be a person or an animal.

It should be noted that during the story, each character can have more than one role and can move between roles as the story progresses.

CHARACTERISATION

While 'character' identifies the people in the story and their role in the plot, it is 'characterisation' that gives depth to the character.

Characterisation fulfils the following functions:
- It reveals the characters through their words, thoughts, actions and physical descriptions
- It shows the characters acting and reacting in order to expose their motivations and emotions.

There are two types of characterisation:

a) Direct characterisation (also called Explicit characterisation or Direct presentation)

The storyteller informs the reader what the character is like. The author can do this or can let one of the characters give the details.

b) Indirect characterisation (also called Implicit characterisation or Indirect presentation)

Here the reader must infer what the character is like from the character's words, thoughts and actions. There is no direct description or explicit details of their motivation.

Summary

Characterisation increased in popularity from the nineteenth century onwards. Readers became more interested in why characters did things and wanted to know more about the way they reacted. Motivation and character response took precedence over plot.

Characterisation enables the audience to empathise with the characters in the story. They share the character's experiences. The audience becomes involved and involvement maintains your audience's interest.

Chapter 13

TERMINOLOGY:
Traits, Character traits, Character, Personality traits, Personality, Temperament

In the previous chapter, you met characterisation where the author gives information about the characters directly or indirectly. The details can include dialogue, thoughts and actions. The purpose is to help the audience learn more about the characters and their motivation. In this chapter you will learn about traits, character traits, character, personality traits, personality and temperament.

TRAITS

Early mankind used their senses to interpret and understand the world around them.

With the onset of words and language, mankind was able to describe their own and another person's actions. More importantly, mankind could give labels to abstract qualities. The character who killed the lion was now 'brave', 'courageous' or 'gallant'. The person who gave false information was 'deceitful', 'untrustworthy' or 'evil'.

The more mankind saw the actions of others, the greater the collection of words. The list of traits to describe those actions grew. Traits were actions, that people saw. They were descriptions of a person's physical behaviour. They were adjectives.

Positive trait adjectives included: adventurous; capable; caring; fearless, and reliable.

Negative trait adjectives included: cowardly; dishonest; lazy, and unfriendly.

As time moved on and language developed, the number of traits grew. Mankind accumulated an arsenal of traits.

CHARACTER TRAITS

It is important to distinguish between traits and character traits. Traits are individual concepts; they stand alone.

Character traits are a group of traits that identify a character. By combining traits, a writer can add another dimension to the character.

Character traits can be implicit or explicit. They can change. You learn about a person's character traits by watching how they interact with the world. They are used to describe how characters act in certain situations or how they respond. They reveal what kind of people they are.

Character traits can change. They are used to describe, not explain, how a character acts or reacts.

CHARACTER

Character is the intellectual, conscious dimension of mankind. It is the result of man's conscious effort to modify certain aspects of his innate temperament by using his intellectual and emotional faculties and will-power. It is a synthesis of all the particular characteristics of a man's temperament that have been brought under control.

Character is formed by the conscious tendencies of a person who reasons and reflects. This results in an attitude, a way of manifesting oneself, which often contradicts one's basic temperament. It is a new version of their temperament. It has been modified. It is a deliberately acquired habit. It is not inborn, and it is formed gradually over a number of years.

PERSONALITY TRAITS

While character traits are simple, personality traits are complex.

Personality traits are how the author explains the way a person thinks and behaves most of the time. Personality traits interact with each other and are more stable and permanent than character traits. Personality traits are more consistent over time. They are more consistent from one situation to another. Personality traits are innate and cause behaviour, while character traits are a reaction to an external stimulus. You are born with personality traits. You acquire character traits.

A trait is a personality trait when:
- It is consistent in all situations (person worries at home and also worries at work)
- It is stable over time (person worries when twenty years old and worries when forty years old)

- It allows for individual differences, i.e. people can have the same trait but with different degrees of intensity (concerned, more concerned, very concerned).

Each personality trait is a specific pattern. This pattern results from a combination of internal experiences and behaviour where the internal experiences involve thinking and feeling.

PERSONALITY

Personality arises from within an individual and remains constant throughout life. It is composed of behaviour (actions), feelings (emotions) and thoughts (cognition). However, it can be acquired and is influenced by education and society.

A group of personality traits make up your 'personality'. Personality enables you to predict what a person will do in a given situation. It helps you to understand why they might have behaved that way.

Personality and personality traits remain constant throughout life.

TEMPERAMENT

Temperament refers to the emotional activity of a person. Temperament is innate. It is inborn. It is not learned. It is a natural instinct – but it can be nurtured.

Temperament is the synthesis of all your instincts, tendencies and impulses which humans are incapable of changing or eliminating because they are rooted in your biological and physiological make-up. These tendencies lie beneath the surface of your consciousness. Temperament is closely related to your animal nature.

Temperament is impossible to change. You are born with your temperament. It has been clearly defined in advance.

Personality traits and temperament show a degree of correlation.

Chapter 14

TERMINOLOGY:
Myths, Legends, Folklore, Folktales, Fairy Tales

MYTHS

A myth is a traditional story that tries to answer many of life's important questions. The purpose of a myth is to explain.

A myth explains the reasons why things have come to be, why the world looks the way it does and why it works the way it does. Myths are an attempt to tell the audience how events, practices and beliefs came about. They were originally intended to provide meaning and order in a chaotic world.

A myth tries to explain mysteries, supernatural events or cultural traditions. It can involve gods, heroes, humans and animals in various settings accomplishing supernatural feats. It presents reality in dramatic ways. Myths are not based on historical facts.

Myths were used to help the audience know the unknown. They explained origins, demystified supernatural events and presented reality in a sensational way using gods and amazing creatures. They were attempts to explain creation, divinity, religion and the meaning of life and death.

Some myths were concerned with the early history of a race of people. They specified lineage, names, status and property rights. They also described the origins of a person, place, natural phenomena and social origins. These were all the things that were important to the social group in which the myth was told.

LEGENDS

A legend is a narrative of actions performed by humans some time in history.

The purpose of a legend is usually to teach certain virtues and inspire an audience. While myths explain, legends teach.

They are woven around historical figures who are considered heroes despite their flaws. A legend is often an account of a person or an event in the past that was greatly exaggerated. It can even include supernatural or extraordinary elements.

Much of early literature began as legends. Originally the legends were told orally in epic poems. At a later date, they were written down. Legends have a significant meaning in the culture in which they arise.

FOLKLORE

Folklore contains all the stories, beliefs and superstitions of a specific culture.

It is a collection of fictional tales about people or animals. These tales were circulated orally and include the superstitions and beliefs that were important to each culture.

The characters can be ordinary humans in unrealistic situations.

Folklore includes folktales and fairy tales.

FOLKTALES

Folktales are stories that reflect simple social situations. They were told by ordinary people rather than aristocrats.

The purpose of the folktale is to teach people how to cope with life and how to behave. They contain a moral or lesson.

Folktales revolve around ordinary fears and desires. They involve some sort of conflict that relates to events in everyday life. They describe how the main character triumphs despite the circumstances.

The characters in the folktale can be humans or supernatural beings such as witches, giants and ogres. The stories often feature contests to win a bride or attempts to overcome wicked stepmothers or sisters.

The origin of many folktales is unknown. They were created orally and passed on by word of mouth. There can be many versions of the same tale.

FAIRY TALES

Fairy tales feature ordinary human beings in extraordinary situations. They include magical beings and are set in faraway kingdoms or forests. The events happened a long time ago.

Fairy tales were originally told orally in aristocratic society. Their purpose was to entertain.

Eventually, they were written down then modified for children. The purpose changed from entertainment to teaching. The fairy tale became a story intended to teach the child a moral lesson.

Fairy tales are part of the folklore tradition. They can share the same elements as folktales.

SUMMARY

A **myth** is a traditional story that tries to answer many of life's important questions. The purpose of a myth is to explain.

A **legend** is a narrative of actions performed by humans sometime in history. The purpose of a legend is to teach certain virtues and inspire an audience.

Folklore is all the stories, beliefs, superstitions that embody a specific culture. Folklore includes folktales and fairy tales.

Folktales are stories that reflect simple social situations and were told by ordinary people rather than aristocrats. The purpose of the folktale is to teach people how to cope with life and how to behave. They contain a moral or lesson.

Fairy tales feature ordinary human beings in extraordinary situations. They include magical beings and are set in faraway kingdoms or forests. The events happened a long time ago.
Their purpose originally was to entertain adults. Their purpose changed and was intended to teach children a moral lesson.

Chapter 15

TERMINOLOGY:
Fables, Parables, Sagas, Epics

FABLES

Fables are instructive tales that teach morals about human social behaviour.

Fables feature personified animals or natural objects. The context does not specify the time or the place. They are entirely fictional. Fables are intended to teach lessons and morals. The topics concern truths about life.

PARABLES

A parable is a tale that illustrates a doctrine or a standard of conduct.

The topic is usually of a religious or spiritual nature. It is designed to teach important lessons about life. While fables use animals, plants, inanimate objects and forces of Nature as characters, the parable features human characters.

SAGA

A saga is an extended narrative that recreates historical events.

It is firmly grounded in a specific historical setting. The word *saga* has its origins in the Middle Ages. In those days, a saga was a historical tale of the first families who lived in Norway or Iceland. Nowadays, the word is used to describe a very complicated or detailed series of events. A saga is a long and drawn-out story.

EPIC

Epics are not confined to a particular time or place. They use poetry to express the story. They celebrate heroic feats.

Epics are similar to sagas in that they refer to historical events. They differ in that epics use poetry and can involve mythical people and events.

Chapter 16

TERMINOLOGY:
Plot story, Character story, Personal story, Business story, Short story, Flash fiction

PLOT STORY

Plot-driven stories focus on the choices that a character has to make rather than on how the character arrives at that choice.

Plot-driven writing is focused on the actual events and the external changes of the story. It places greater emphasis on the plot itself. Factors such as plot twists, action and external conflict are important in this style of writing. In most cases, the goals of the story are more external in that they are focused on the development of a situation. In plot-driven novels, the characters are usually forced to make quick decisions and, as a result, the development of the characters takes a back seat to the rapidly evolving story.

CHARACTER STORY

Character-driven stories deal with the inner transformation of the character. They can also deal with the relationships between the characters. They focus on how the character arrives at a particular choice.

Character-driven writing is focused on the characters and internal changes, rather than external events and situations. It focuses on the inner conflict of the characters. The audience will spend time thinking about the characters and their attitudes and decisions, and how those character decisions changed the shape of the plot and the story as a whole.

Character-driven stories are commonly referred to as 'literary fiction' because they feature characters that possess many layers that are exposed during the story.

PERSONAL STORY

The personal story provides you with an opportunity to share a meaningful event from your life.

A personal narrative can focus on any event, whether it is one that lasted a few seconds or spanned a few years. Your topic can reflect your personality, or it can reveal an event that shaped your outlooks and opinions. When you recount your personal story, you should imagine that you are re-living the event. You describe what you saw, smelled, heard and felt. The most important thing is that your story should have a clear point and come to a satisfying end.

BUSINESS STORY

Business stories have emerged as a prominent trend in the business world as organisations look to enhance brand awareness and loyalty by telling compelling stories about their products and services. Television commercials often use a story to position their products and services.

Employees who develop a compelling business story have a better chance of progressing within the organisation and increasing their salary. Business stories can help you to paint a dynamic picture of your achievements and the way you overcame obstacles. In an interview situation, they provide concrete examples of how you made a difference at work. Business stories are the most engaging and convincing way to convey proof that you have made an impact in a business context.

SHORT STORY

A short story is brief fictional prose narrative that is shorter than a novel. It usually deals with only a few characters. It often concentrates on the creation of mood rather than plot.

Because of the shorter length, a short story usually focuses on one plot, one main character (with a few additional minor characters) and one central theme. Short stories also lend themselves more to experimentation. They may use unusual prose styles or literary devices to tell the story. Such styles or devices might get tedious in a novel, but they may work well in a short story.

FLASH FICTION

Flash fiction is a short form of storytelling.

Defining the term by the number of words or sentences (or even pages) required to tell a story is impossible because the definition of flash fiction differs from writer to writer and, editor to editor. Some purists insist that it is a complete story told in less than 75 words; others claim 100 should be the maximum. Some authors consider anything under 1,000 words can be flash-worthy. There are even a few who stretch the limits to 1,500 words.

Part poetry, part narrative, flash fiction is also known as 'sudden fiction', 'micro fiction', 'short, short stories' and 'quick fiction'.

By definition, flash fiction begins at the moment of conflict when all the action is nearly complete. This avoids preambles or introductions. It focuses on more powerful images and finishes with an ending that offers an emotional impact.

Chapter 17

TERMINOLOGY:
Beliefs, Values, Attitudes, Opinions, Prejudices

BELIEFS

Beliefs are assumptions and convictions that people accept as being true.

They can be based on certainties or on probabilities. They can be based on facts, opinions or assumptions. They can be based on what you have been told, on what you have observed or on what you have experienced.

You hold on to your beliefs regardless of facts or evidence to the contrary. You want them to be true and are not concerned with their validity.

Beliefs form your 'belief system', which guides your actions and behaviour. You use this belief system to make decisions about the future. You will defend your belief system because you are convinced that it is correct, and you do not want to contradict yourself. You certainly do not want to prove yourself wrong.

Beliefs influence your behaviour.

VALUES

Values are standards by which people order their lives and make choices. They enable you to make moral choices. You use values to make your decisions.

Values start as beliefs. When the commitment to the belief grows and it becomes important to the person, it becomes a value for that person.

Values are influenced by your background, experiences and the society in which you live. You often incorporate society's values into your own system. A culture's values relate to the ideal society and are aspirations that you should embrace, such as moral behaviour.

Values are based on what is important to you. They relate to your needs. As your important needs change, so do your values. You use values to make your decisions.

Values can change, while your beliefs are more resistant to change.

ATTITUDES

An attitude is a predisposition or a tendency to respond positively or negatively toward a certain idea, object, person, or situation.

Attitudes are formed from underlying beliefs and values. People who do not have strong beliefs or values about a topic tend to form attitudes much more quickly. These attitudes are less rational and change quickly. As a result, their behaviour can change quickly also.

Attitudes have three components:

a) Affective (Emotional) =
how the object/person/issue/event makes you feel.

b) Cognitive (Reasoning) =
how attitude influences your thoughts and beliefs about the object/person/issue/event.

c) Behavioural (Conative) =
how the attitude influences your behaviour. The combination of your feeling and thinking about the object/person/issue/event leads you to act in a certain way.

Attitude can have three dimensions:

i) Attitude strength =
attitudes that are firmly held have a big influence on your behaviour. These attitudes concern topics that you know a lot about and are important to you.

ii) Attitude accessibility =
this refers to the ease with which the attitude comes to mind. Highly accessible attitudes are much stronger.

iii) Attitude ambivalence =
this refers to the ratio of positive and negative evaluations that make up the attitude. The ambivalence of an attitude increases

as the positive and negative evaluations get more and more equal.

Attitude can be explicit or implicit:

Explicit attitudes =
attitudes that you are aware of and clearly influence your beliefs, decisions and behaviour.

Implicit attitudes =
Attitudes that you are unconscious of but still influence your beliefs, decisions and behaviour.
Attitudes are dynamic in nature. They can keep changing depending on your experiences. As a result, the more experiences you have, the more your attitude about the object/person/issue/event can change.

Opinion

Opinion is a view or judgement that you form about an object/person/issue/event. It is not based on fact or knowledge. It cannot be disproved or contested in a rational or logical manner.

Opinions are influenced by your attitudes and your attitudes are formed by your underlying beliefs and values. While attitudes predispose us to act, opinion is concerned with your evaluation or judgement of the object/person/issue/event.

Opinion is changeable, depending on how you interpret the evidence.

Prejudice

Prejudice is a statement that is not based on sufficient evidence. It can be contested and disproved on the basis of facts.

Prejudice is opinion that is not based on reason or actual experience.

Prejudice can have a strong influence on how people behave and interact with others, particularly with those who are different from them. Prejudice is a baseless, and usually negative, attitude toward members of a group. Common features of prejudice include negative feelings, stereotyped beliefs and a tendency to discriminate against members of the group. While specific definitions of prejudice given by social scientists often differ, most agree that it involves prejudgments about members of a group that are usually negative.

When people hold prejudicial attitudes toward others, they tend to view everyone who fits into a certain group as being 'all the same'. They paint every individual who holds particular characteristics or beliefs with a very broad brush and fail to look at each person as a unique individual.

Types

Prejudice can be based on a number of factors including sex, race, age, sexual orientation, nationality, socio-economic status, and religion. Some of the most well-known types of prejudice include:
- Racism
- Sexism
- Classicism

- Homophobia
- Nationalism
- Religious prejudice
- Ageism
- Xenophobia.

Summary

Beliefs are assumptions and convictions that you accept as being true. You hold on to your beliefs regardless of facts or evidence to the contrary. Beliefs influence your behaviour. Beliefs are resistant to change.

Values start as beliefs. Once established, they are standards by which you order your life and make choices. You use values to make your decisions. Values can change while your beliefs are resistant to change.

Attitudes are formed from your underlying beliefs and values. Attitudes are a tendency to respond positively or negatively toward an object/person/issue/event.

Opinion is influenced by your attitude. Opinion is a view or judgement that you form about an object/person/issue/event. While attitude predisposes you to act, opinion is concerned about your evaluation of the object/person/issue/event.

Prejudice is an opinion that is not based on reason or experience. Prejudice is not based on sufficient evidence and can be disproved on the basis of facts.

CONCLUSION

Before the evolution of language, people were concerned about survival. This was instinctive, it was innate. Survival of self and the survival of the species dominated man's actions. There were struggles, there was success, there was survival. Initially, animals and Nature were mankind's greatest threat. As societies developed, man himself became the threat.

With a language to describe events, the early stories helped the hunter to simulate the hunt. The audience would listen intently and learn how to stay safe while conquering the beast. Words were a means of informing.

The first stories always involved people. People were at the centre of stories from the outset. People hunting animals. People reacting to Nature. People fighting people. People and conflict were at the centre of every story. People and conflict become part of the human psyche. They are part of the collective unconscious that you and your audience have inherited

Stories developed from simply describing an event to using literary techniques to heighten the tension. Events would include a situation that could have many outcomes. The audience would guess a possible choice then await the announcement of the character's decision. Descriptions of events got longer. Adjectives helped intensify the dangers and the thrills. Characters were added and sub-plots were introduced. The simple story grew into a storyline worthy of Hollywood.

The purpose of this book has been to identify the minimum elements you need to create a story that will resonate with the largest audience. The elements are not based on modern literary decrees. They are based on human nature, the psyche of mankind and the findings of psychologists.

Use this book to identify those elements of a story that all can relate to and produce a script that will entertain the world.

References

ARCHETYPES

Anne Baring, *The Dream of the Cosmos*, UK, Archive Publishing, 2013

Joseph Campbell, *The Hero with a Thousand Faces*, CA, New World Library, 2008

Joseph Campbell, *The Masks of God, Volume 1: Primitive Mythology*, New York, The Viking Press, 1959

Carl Jung, *The Structure and Dynamics of the Psyche*, London, Routledge and Kegan Paul Ltd, 1960

Carl Jung, *The Archetypes and the Collective Unconscious*, 2nd ed, *The Collective Work of C.G. Jung,* vol 9. Part 1, New Jersey, Princeton University Press, 1968

Keiron Le Grice, *Archetypal Reflections*, London, Muswell Hill Press, 2016

Caroline Myss, *Archetypes*, London, Hay House UK Ltd, 2013

Marie-Louise Von Franz, *Archetypal Patterns in Fairy Tales*, Toronto, Inner City Books, 1997

Christopher Vogler, *The Writer's Journey*, CA, Michael Wiese Productions, 1992

http://www.soulcraft.co/essays/the_12_common_archetypes.html

http://thewriterspot.weebly.com/miscellaneous/common-character-archetypes

CHARACTERS

https://learn.lexiconic.net/characters.htm
http://literarydevices.com/characterization/
https://study.com/academy/lesson/character-in-literature-definition-types-development.html

http://www.softschools.com/examples/grammar/characterizatio
n_examples/2008/

CURIOSITY
Daniel Berlyne, *Conflict, Arousal and Curiosity*, New York,
McGraw Hill Book Company Inc, 1960
Daniel Berlyne, *The Arousal and Satisfaction of Perceptual
Curiosity in the Rat*, Journal of Comparative Physiological
Psychology 48:238–246, September 1955
Susan Engel, *The Hungry Mind*, USA, Harvard University
Press, 2015
Ian Leslie, *Curious*, London, Quercus Publishing Ltd, 2015
Mario Livio, *Why*, New York, Simon and Schuster, 2017
George Lowenstein, *The Psychology of Curiosity*, Psychology
Bulletin, 116, 1994 pp75–98
http://www.rochester.edu/newscenter/what-drives-curiosity-
research/

EMOTIONS
Charles Darwin, *The Expression of Emotions in Man and
Animal*, Oxford, Oxford University Press, 1872
Paul Ekman, *Emotions Revealed*, London, Orion Books Ltd,
2004
Giovanni Frazzetto, *How We Feel*, London, Transworld
Publishers, 2013
Martin Kringelbach, *Emotion*, USA, Oxford University Press,
2014
Vikas Gopal Jhingran, *Emote*, USA, The Careers Press, 2014

IMAGINATION

Michael Adams, *For the Love of Imagination*, UK, Routledge, 2014

Susan Engel, *Context is Everything*, New York, W H Freeman and Company, 1999

Susan Engel, *The Hungry Mind*, USA, Harvard University Press, 2015

Elaine Reese, *Tell Me a Story*, USA, Oxford University Press, 2013

Marjorie Taylor, *The Oxford Handbook of the Development of Imagination*, USA, Oxford University Press, 2013

MOTIVATION

Gillian Burn, *Motivation for Dummies*, Chichester, John Wiley and Sons Ltd, 2008

Abraham Maslow, *Motivation and Personality*, New York, Harper and Row Publishers, 1987

https://www.businessballs.com/self-awareness/maslows-hierarchy-of-needs/

NARRATIVE

https://www.bookoblivion.com
https://www.beemgee.com
https://cla.purdue.edu
https://www.nownovel.com/blog/narrative-examples-strong-narration/

PERSONALITY

https://examples.yourdictionary.com/examples-of-personality-traits.html
https://www.verywellmind.com/trait-theory-of-personality2795955
https://www.123test.com/big-five-personality-theory/
https://nobaproject.com/modules/personality-traits
https://www.reference.com/world-view/difference-between-personality-character-1a2d9491584be13b

PLOT

Christopher Booker, *The Seven Basic Plots*, London, Bloomsbury Publishing Plc, 2004
Joseph Campbell, *The Hero with a Thousand Faces*, CA, New World Library, 2008
Georges Polti, *The Thirty-Six Dramatic Situations*, Boston, The Writer Inc, 1916
Christopher Vogler, *The Writer's Journey*, USA, Michael Wiese Publications, 1992

About the author

Paul has been committed to writing since his schooldays. He was the editor of an in-house magazine at school. When the bulletin was thin, he would write articles. After taking many courses, he had several articles published.

His obsession with discovering the elements of a great story led Paul to fairy tales. These concise, dramatic stories have characters and plots that have stood the test of time. What is it about fairy tales that makes them so popular and engaging?

The search led Paul through a maze of research, which resulted in his previous three Amazon books about writing:
Write the story that could make you rich – the formula used to write the top-grossing films and books
How to create a short story quickly and easily – Discover the secret formula used by the master storytellers to get the attention of their audience
Writers: get more readers, make more money – the structure, the plots, the characters used by successful writers.

In *How to Write a Story – an alternative approach using the subconscious*, you will discover another starting point for your story.

Wishing you every success.

www.ingramcontent.com/pod-product-compliance
Lightning Source LLC
Chambersburg PA
CBHW060419290526
45791CB00002B/815